The Mystery of Stonehenge

by Nancy Lyon

A

Book

From

RAINTREE CHILDRENS BOOKS
Milwaukee • Toronto • Melbourne • London

Library of Congress Number: 77-10044

Art and Photo Credits

Cover photo, Gerry Cranham/Photo Researchers, Inc.
Photo on title page and page 16, courtesy of the American Museum of
Natural History.
Photo on page 7, Russ Kinne/Photo Researchers, Inc.
Illustrations on pages 10, 21, 32 and 36, Isadore Seltzer.
Photo on page 12, David Moore/Photo Researchers, Inc.
Photos on pages 19 and 26, Elizabeth H. Burpee/dpi.
Photo on page 24, Jerry Cooke/Photo Researchers, Inc.
Photo on page 28, K. A. Schnitzer/dpi.
Illustrations on pages 29, 30, and 41 courtesy of the New York Public Library
Picture Collection.
Illustration on page 35, courtesy of Collier's Encyclopedia.
Map on page 39, courtesy of Alfred Fusco.
Photos on pages 44 and 47, Wide World Photos.
All photo research for this book was provided by Roberta Guerette.
Every effort has been made to trace the ownership of all copyrighted material in
this book and to obtain permission for its use.

Library of Congress Cataloging in Publication Data

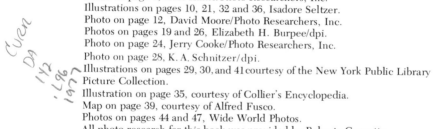

> Lyon, Nancy, 1947-
>   The mystery of Stonehenge
>   SUMMARY: Discusses the theories and superstitions
> that have risen throughout the years to explain
> the existence of the circle of stones at Stonehenge.
>   1. Stonehenge—Juvenile literature. [1. Stone-
> henge] I. Title.
> DA142.L96   913.362   77-10044
> ISBN 0-8172-1049-0 lib. bdg.

Manufactured in the United States of America.
ISBN 0-8172-1049-0

Contents

Chapter 1
   The Mysterious "Circle of Giants"   5

Chapter 2
   Tall Tales of Tall Stones   9

Chapter 3
   Searching for Clues   14

Chapter 4
   Steady Jobs for Forty Generations   18

Chapter 5
   Stonehenge Revealed   23

Chapter 6
   Magical Bluestones and Shapely
   Sarsens   34

Chapter 7
   What Stonehenge Means   43

The Mysterious "Circle of Giants"

You are standing on the flat land of the *Salisbury Plain* in the south of England. The night air is misty. A cold wind slaps your face and moves through the night. The darkness of the plain stretches as far as you can see. *This must be the loneliest place in the world.*

Wait a minute. You are not alone. What are those shapes ahead of you? You shine your flashlight on the dark and looming shapes. They don't move! If the shapes are human, they must be giants. If they are animals, they aren't frightened by the light.

You move closer, but carefully—*very* carefully. It's dark and cold and you are alone. You try to stop your legs from shaking. It's no use. You *know* you are scared!

Suddenly you laugh and shout into the darkness, "They're only stones!"

That's right! You move closer to the towering shapes. They are a *circle* of great stones—forty "giants" standing on end, each one at least four times larger than the tallest human. They seem to reach up from the earth, trying to touch the sky.

What you don't know is that their mysterious shapes have stood stubbornly against howling winds and damp mists for over 4,000 years. They look as if they will stand long after human beings have left the face of the earth.

What are these "giants" all about? Their mystery stops you cold on the spot. It takes your breath away for a brief moment. You decide not to wait until morning to start looking for the answer.

On the way back to the safety of an English inn, a million questions rattle in your head. Why are those stones there—in the middle of no-

The ghostly shapes of Stonehenge in the moonlight.

where? When were they put there? Who could have moved so many tons of rock to this flat, lonely plain?

Barely inside the front door, you decide to find out more about these mystery stones. A local villager gives you some very interesting books. Let's see what they reveal.

The strange circle of stones is called *Stonehenge.* (*Henge* is a form of an Old English word meaning "to hang.") Some say it was given this name because its huge stones almost seem to hang in midair. Others say it is called *Stonehenge* because criminals were once hanged from these very stones. But there is more to this circle than meets the eye. Someone went too far just to hang criminals!

What is known about this strange circle? First fact: Stonehenge is certainly famous. But it is not the only ancient stone circle. Others were built all over Europe. They were built to last for thousands of years, and they did! There are about *50,000* of them standing today. These great *megaliths* (from the Greek word meaning "great stone") look like frozen giants rising from the earth.

Another fact: Scientists show that many of these megaliths were used as tombs. For human skeletons have been buried among the stones. But scientists doubt that this was their only purpose. There they stand—the forty "giants" of Stonehenge—bigger than life. There were no mechanics to lift or move them from far-off places. These stones must have had a very, very special use. But what?

Chapter 2

Tall Tales of Tall Stones

Many stories have been told about the "giants" of Stonehenge and how they got there. Some legends say the stones were giants who were magically turned to stone while they danced. They call the stones "The Giants Dance."

Others say that giants had carried the stones from the farthest reaches of Africa. There was a stop in Ireland. But finally the stones were brought to England. Why all that work? Some say the giants believed that the stones had magical healing powers.

One legend says that Stonehenge was formed when dancing giants were changed to stone.

Another story is that Merlin the Magician waved his magic wand. The stones flew through the air from a mountain in Ireland to their resting place in England.

There is also a tale that the Devil himself put the stones where they are. It seems the mysterious stones were growing in the backyard of an old woman in Ireland. When the Devil heard about the strange stones, he wanted them for himself. Dressed as a gentleman, he went to make the old woman a deal for the stones.

The Devil poured a big pile of coins on the woman's table, right before her eyes. As soon as she saw the money, she agreed to sell the stones. All the while, she thought, "It will take this man forever to move those stones." As she reached for the coins, the Devil said, "Hold! The stones are gone."

Sure enough, the stones had disappeared! The Devil had already spirited them away to the Salisbury Plain where they stand today.

Pleased with his trick, the Devil bragged to his friends that nobody would ever be able to tell how many stones were brought there. But an old friar overheard the Devil's boast and cried out, "That is more than thee canst tell."

The Devil became very angry with the friar and threw one of the stones at him. It landed on the friar's heel. The friar was so strong that his heel dented the stone. The friar's Heel Stone still stands at Stonehenge.

Modern legends of Stonehenge are told the world over. Some people say that the prehistoric people knew about the magnetic currents of the earth. These currents were used to make heavy objects fly. Maybe these people used the stones as "flying carpets" to go from place to place.

Others believe that Stonehenge was built by people from a continent called *Atlantis* which sank into the sea thousands of years ago.

Giant shadows cast by giant stones.

Still another modern tale is that the stones were put on Salisbury Plain by creatures from outer space! But like the legend of the old friar, these modern beliefs have no basis in fact.

In the last 50 years, while people have gone over these strange stories, scientists have gone over every inch of the strange stones.

Like the legends and tall tales, the mystery grows and grows. Who will unlock the secrets of Stonehenge—what it was, and why it was built?

Chapter 3

Searching for Clues

Of all the prehistoric stone monuments, Stonehenge is the most interesting. Its stones are carefully shaped to different sizes, fitted together, and placed in a special pattern.

Was Stonehenge a sacred temple where human sacrifices were offered to the gods? Maybe. Was it a star observatory? Perhaps. A gigantic calendar? It's possible. Was it a great marketplace? Some think so. Or was it simply a giant cattle pen? Who knows? The builders of Stonehenge left no clues.

14

The riddles of Stonehenge have puzzled scientists and engineers from all parts of the world. They are slowly putting together the pieces of this great puzzle. The story the pieces tell is even more amazing than the Stonehenge legends.

The first piece in the puzzle must be the answer to the question, "How old is Stonehenge?" Scientists must know exactly how old Stonehenge is. Without a pinpoint in history, they can't narrow down the possible reasons why Stonehenge was built.

To figure out its age, scientists first looked for tools buried near the giant stones. They found picks and rakes made from deer antlers, and shovels made from the shoulder blades of oxen. *Radiocarbon dating* was used to measure the age of these ancient tools. This method even reveals the age of ashes from fires lit there long ago.

In the late 1940s, Willard Libby, an American chemist, found that all living things have atoms of *carbon 14*. When living creatures die, their bodies decay. So do the atoms of carbon 14. The rate of decay of carbon 14 tells how much time has passed since the body's death. Special machines read this "clock of decay" and tell scientists the age of things that died long ago.

By measuring the rate of decay of carbon 14, this special
equipment tells scientists the age of things that died long ago.

According to carbon 14 dating, the tools
under special study were made in 2700 B.C. But
who made these tools?

The next step in research was carried out
by archaeologists (scientists who study the remains of ancient civilizations). In the Stonehenge

area, they dug up ashes of human bodies buried in animal skin bags. They also uncovered long-buried jewelry, weapons, and tools. All these told the archaeologists that Stonehenge was built over a long period of time, by different groups of people, and in three different stages.

Who were these people? The mystery of Stonehenge was still far from being solved. Everything in the area had to be carefully examined for clues to the next piece in the puzzle.

Chapter 4

Steady Jobs for Forty Generations

The stone circles of ancient Europe were built by different people over a period of 3,000 years. Because of the giant stones they used, these builders have been named "Megalith People."

Megalith People throughout Europe had similar lifestyles and, for some reason, they shared an interest in building giant stone circles and monuments.

Monuments like Stonehenge were built all over Europe. Here are the remains of a burial tomb in Cornwall, England.

The first Megalith People who worked on Stonehenge were called Wessex People. (Stonehenge is located in a part of England called Wessex.) They probably came to the Salisbury Plain from many different countries.

Archaeologists have put together a picture of what life was like for these earliest builders of Stonehenge. The Wessex People lived together in small groups of 50 people. They stayed in one

19

place until they could no longer raise enough crops to feed themselves. When they moved on, they took their animals, tools, and cooking utensils with them. In the spring, they set up tents covered with animal skins. Later, they would build strong houses of wood. They planted wheat and barley; they fished and hunted.

Archaeologists have dug up many stone tools in the areas where the Wessex People lived. When the Wessex People started to build Stonehenge, the civilization of Egypt was already thousands of years old. Travelers from these places may have told the people of Wessex about their own inventions and discoveries. Maybe that's how the Wessex People learned to make the stone tools that they needed to build Stonehenge.

It took over 3,000 years just to complete Stonehenge. In the lifetime of one builder, only a small amount of progress could be seen. A person might work every day for a whole lifetime just to shape, carry, and put a few stones in place!

Imagine spending your whole life building something you can never hope to see finished? What could have kept these people on the job? You have a right to ask such questions! Were these people slaves with no choice but to work on Stonehenge? Were they afraid to displease the gods who ordered the stone circles to be built? No one knows. But it seems that it would have

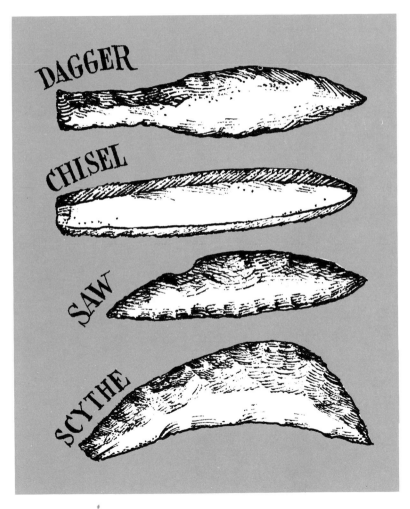

These are samples of simple tools used by the Megalith people.

been easy for slaves to escape if they had not wanted to work. Probably Stonehenge was built by people who *wanted* to build it—forty generations of such people!

Scientists believe the builders of Stonehenge had a great knowledge of mathematics and engineering. How else could they have placed the stones in positions that reflect the movements of the sun and moon? How else could they have carried and lifted such huge stones without the use of modern tools and machines?

Chapter 5

Stonehenge Revealed

What is left of Stonehenge today is only a ruin. Some of the pieces have fallen over. The great stones lie on the ground like dead warriors. Other stones have broken or are missing. Some were broken apart over the centuries by people who thought the stones were reminders of the evil past. They believed that Stonehenge was built to honor animal gods. During the Middle Ages, this "megalith wrecking" became a super-stitious ceremony. Every 25 years, a giant stone was thrown down to "throw out the Devil."

Other pieces of Stonehenge were broken up and carted away by souvenir hunters. That was before England decided to protect Stonehenge as a monument for all time. In fact, at one time, a large hammer was kept hanging from one of the big stones. The hammer was to help tourists chip away pieces of Stonehenge.

Because of the way the remaining stones were placed, you can piece together a picture of

All that remains of Stonehenge today is this broken circle of stones.

the great stone circle that once stood in the Salisbury Plain. Remember, Stonehenge consisted of more than just stones. And remember that the building was done over 3,000 years!

During the first of the three building periods (called Stonehenge I), two raised earth circles were placed 300 feet from each other. Between the circles was a wide ditch. The soil of Salisbury Plain was chalky and white. So circles of earth must have been visible for miles around. But the circles have been worn down through the ages. Today they are covered with soft grass.

There is an opening on the northeast side of the Stonehenge walls. Through that opening runs a roadway that continues to the river Avon, two miles away. This roadway is called the *Avenue*.

In the middle of the Avenue, near the edge of the wide circle, is the oldest and most famous stone of Stonehenge. It's called the *Heel Stone*. Remember? This is the stone that the Devil was said to have thrown at the friar. It stands 15 feet high and weighs over 35 tons. The Heel Stone was probably the first stone of Stonehenge.

The rest of Stonehenge I is a circle of 56 holes inside the earth circles. These are called the

The dented Heel Stone—the first stone of Stonehenge.

Aubrey holes, named for John Aubrey who discovered them in 1648. Animal skin bags filled with human ashes were found in the holes. This supports the idea that Stonehenge may have been a burial ground.

Four tall stones stand on the faint circle of the Aubrey holes. Each stone has a ditch around

26

it. These are the *Station Stones,* and they form a perfect rectangle. Draw lines along the rectangle, or draw diagonally across it. On certain days, such lines point to the rising of the sun and moon. Was Stonehenge also an observatory for the stars? Were the people who built Stonehenge astronomers?

Inside the circle of Aubrey holes is a big circle of sandstones—the *Sarsen Circle.* It was built during Stonehenge III, the last building period. It is a ring of tall stones with stone roofs.

Inside the sandstone circle is one more circle that is quite different. The stones in this circle are bluish in color. Each bluestone stands alone. These were placed in the circle during the middle period of construction, Stonehenge II.

Inside the bluestone circle is the great horseshoe. It was built as five pairs of roofed stones. In front of the central roofed stone is the *Altar Stone.* Some say the Altar Stone is stained with the blood of sacrificial victims.

Again you ask, "Who were the builders of these fantastic stone circles? Were they wild-eyed 'witch doctors' dressed in animal skin robes who offered sacrifices to their gods? Were

Without modern engineering, ancient people worked centuries
to move stones many times their own size.

they great engineers and astronomers? Why did
they need a Stonehenge?" Despite all the clues
that have been gathered, the mystery deepens;
the puzzle seems less near completion.

Imagine that you are stepping back in time, almost 5,000 years (into Stonehenge I). Perhaps this is what the building of Stonehenge was like.

Stonehenge may have measured time by the movement of the earth. The solid line shows the path of the sun's rays 4,000 years ago. The dotted line shows the path—same hour, same season—in the 20th century. The slight difference is due to the change in the earth's tilt over thousands of years.

The year is 2750 B.C. (Stonehenge I). After many months of meeting and planning, a group has gathered on the Salisbury Plain. Everyone in the community knows the much awaited day has finally arrived! Men and women carry a long, heavy oxhide rope to the center of the stone circle they plan to build. They drive a huge wooden peg into the earth. One end of the rope is tied to the peg. Two of the men slowly unwind the rope until it is stretched to its full length.

At the rope's end, one of the men ties a deer antler and scratches a deep mark in the earth. Look how white and chalky the earth is where he

When Stonehenge was completed, it may have looked very much like this modern drawing.

has scratched away the dark topsoil. Now, with the rope pulled tight, the same two men move slowly in a circle. They scratch deep marks into the earth with the point of the antler until they come back around to the very first mark. They have scratched a perfect white circle. The peg and rope are a simple compass.

A woman standing nearby leans over to her little son and explains why the men have drawn the gigantic circle. "It will be the outer border of the great circle of stones," she says.

Suddenly a great many of the men and women who, until now, have only been watching, begin to scurry about. Each scoops up a tool. Some carry heavy bones that could be shovels; others carry animal antlers or sharp rocks—pick-axes perhaps? They all move to the white line in the earth and strike at the soil with their crude tools. What a moment! You have just seen the ground broken for the building of one of the great wonders of all time—Stonehenge!

By mid-afternoon, however, you ask yourself if these people understand the job they have cut out for themselves. Never have you seen people work so hard, so long, to get so little done. The soft topsoil hides a hard chalky soil beneath.

Working with crude tools, men and women built a mound six feet high for the stone circle.

Cracking and digging the chalk to form a trench looks as though it will take forever.

By 4 P.M., these people have been working 9 hours. Yet the strongest looking man you can find in the group seems to have dug only about a cubic yard of chalk. The goal is to complete the trench and a six-foot high ridge of earth within the circle. They will have to dig many more yards!

As they dig, they pour each backbreaking scoop of soil and chalk into large baskets. They empty the baskets onto the pile that is building on the inside border of the trench. Several people smooth the pile of chalk and sod into a mound about six feet high. The mound will be a border for the stone circle that is planned.

To see the finished Stonehenge, you would have to remain on the Salisbury Plain for 3,000 more years! But you know that's impossible. You will simply have to keep on asking good questions as you read about Stonehenge II—the most remarkable building of all time!

Chapter 6

Magical Bluestones and Shapely Sarsens

Archaeologists say that the building of Stonehenge stopped for about 200 years after the mound was completed. The Aubrey holes, Heel Stone, and four station stones were also built before all work mysteriously stopped. There are not many details about what happened during the two centuries when no one worked on Stonehenge. But we now know the work began again when some new people—the *Beaker People*—came to the Salisbury Plain.

34

The completed Stonehenge (1) the Heel Stone, (2) the two circles of earth, (3) the Aubrey Holes, (4) the Station Stone, (5) the Sarsen Circle, (6) the Bluestone Circle, (7) the Great Horseshoe, (8) the Atlas Stone.

The newcomers were called the Beaker People because they made bell-shaped, reddish-brown drinking cups. Later these cups were called beakers. The Beaker People also brought bronze tools to the Salisbury Plain.

During Stonehenge II, the bluestones were erected. What's so important about the bluestones, you ask? Only that they could have come from *just one place* in all the world. That place is the Prescelly Mountains in Wales. They are found nowhere else. The Prescelly Mountains are located 130 miles away from Stonehenge! Somehow, the ancient builders of Stonehenge carried 82 of these bluestones, which weighed up to 5 tons each, over land and sea, to the Salisbury Plain.

The Beaker People moved the bluestones on rolling logs.

36

It took many years and many lives to move these bluestones. *Why* didn't the Beaker People use stones that were close by. *Why* did the builders risk their lives to bring these bluestones 25 miles over land and 215 miles over stormy sea?

The Beaker People may have believed the bluestones had magical powers and could heal disease. They may have believed the stones were sacred and held spirits of their dead ancestors. Legend has it that King Arthur himself convinced the Beaker People to move the sacred stones to Salisbury Plain.

Before the bluestones were brought from the Prescelly Mountains, they had to be cut down and shaped. *How* was this done without dynamite and modern chisels?

Scientists believe the heavy bluestones were cut by *cracking* them. First, the workers scratched deep lines where they wanted to break the stones. Then they soaked dried cattails in animal fat to make them burn easily. The cattails were placed along the scratches and set on fire. After the fire was out, cold water was poured along the heated line. Eventually, this combination of heat and cold caused the rock to crack along the line. Wood wedges and heavy rocks widened the crack and finally split the huge stone.

Now the Beaker People were faced with the biggest problem of all. How were they to *move* these tons of stones? Someone thought of an answer—the stones could be *rolled* over land to the sea. The bluestones were tied onto sleds which were pulled along over round wood logs.

As soon as the sled passed over one of the rollers, the round log was carried to the front to move the sled a little further. Moving over a few rollers at a time, the sled with its stone cargo inched its way for 25 miles to the sea. The line of workers pulling the ropes of the sled and moving the heavy rollers must have stretched farther than the eye could see!

Eighty-two of these bluestones, weighing five tons each, were broken free, shaped, and lashed onto the sleds. It would have taken a full day for 80 men to move one stone one mile. To move the 82 stones from the mountain to the sea, the 80 men would have pulled and strained for 2,000 days—almost 6 years. And this was only the first part of the journey. The rest of it—215 miles—had to be made over water.

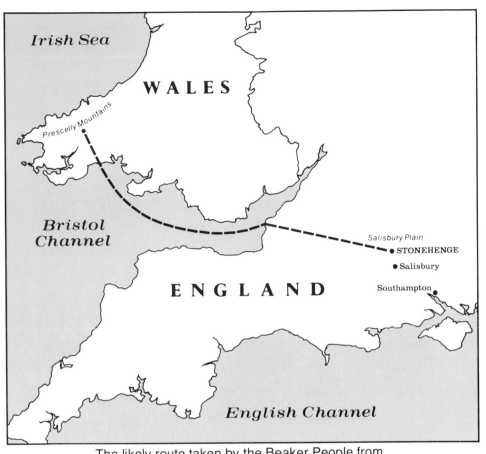

The likely route taken by the Beaker People from
the Prescelly Mountains to the Salisbury Plain.

The giant stones had to be floated across the
rough waters of what is now called the Bristol
Channel that flows from the Irish Sea. Once
across the water, the stones were hauled over
rollers again to the Salisbury Plain.

When they reached the sea, the Beaker
People dug out thick tree trunks to make canoes.

Then they tied together a few of the canoes to form a large raft. The bluestones were dragged onto the rafts. A sail made of thin animal skin was used to catch the wind. A good many people and stones probably never made it over the water. They were lost at sea, the victims of strong currents.

The Beaker People were willing to fight the sea because carrying the stones over water was faster than over land. With good winds, ten people could paddle or sail a raft ten miles a day.

No one really knows how many people worked together at any one time moving the bluestones from Wales to the Salisbury Plain. Modern engineers figure it would have taken *110 men working every day for 540 years* to pull those 82 bluestones over the land portion of the trip. Each stone was finally dragged over rollers to Salisbury Plain from the sea. Compared with this incredible effort, the work to build a skyscraper is like "pitching a tent."

Once on the Salisbury Plain, each stone was slid down ramps and set into a hole about eight feet deep. The space around the stone was then packed tightly with earth and stones. One by one, the bluestones were put into place along the cir-

Stonehenge
as it probably was. Plan & Bird'seye View.

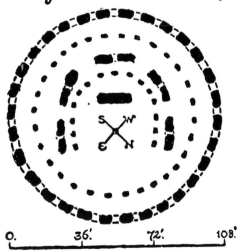

0.   36'   72'   108'

The circle of stones on the Salisbury Plain is 108 feet in diameter.

cle. This took many years. Probably no worker
ever lived to see more than 20 of them in place.
The Beaker People who had worked so long and

hard could only *imagine* what Stonehenge would finally look like.

Some of the "trickiest" work on Stonehenge was yet to come. During Stonehenge III, the Sarsen Stones, weighing 40 tons each, had to be dragged from the Marlborough Downs, some 20 miles to the north. It took 1,000 men at least 7 years to move all these huge sandstones to Salisbury Plain. They needed 1,000 workers to move just one of these stones! But after moving the stones into place, an even harder job began. Each of the Sarsens had to be capped with a stone roof.

The Sarsen Stones were very hard rock. Each stone had to be shaped and measured very carefully. For each standing stone, another had to be cut so that it could be lifted and balanced atop the standing stone, as a roof. The roof stones had to be curved slightly, so they would fit into a circle. The edges of the roof stones had to be shaped to fit into each other so they would not slide off the standing stones.

How these roof stones were ever lifted onto the tops of the standing stones, remains a secret. But one mistake—just one—and the roof stone could slip to crush the bodies of dozens of workers.

Chapter 7

What Stonehenge Means

Just why was Stonehenge built? The best clue to this mystery comes from the stones themselves. Astronomer Gerald Hawkins of Boston University visited Stonehenge in the 1960s. He took many measurements of the stones, fed the figures to a computer, and arrived at a theory about why Stonehenge was built.

The sun and the moon were very important to Stone Age people. When the sun or moon suddenly disappeared from the sky during an eclipse, the people became very frightened. They thought that the sun and moon were angry with them.

In the traditional white robe, a modern-day Druid celebrates the
beginning of summer.

The priests and kings of these tribes knew that if they could predict when an eclipse would occur, they would be greatly respected. They would also hold great power over the people, for they would seem to control the sun and the moon. Hawkins believes Stonehenge was built to predict the eclipses of the sun and moon. He believes that Stonehenge was a giant observatory. But was it?

For the last hundred years, one of the most popular beliefs has been that Stonehenge was built by the Druids for study and worship. The Druids were the priests, doctors, and wise men of the Celts, an ancient tribe who lived in England. The Druids studied astronomy and they worshipped nature. They worshipped the sky, mountains, lakes, and all animals.

The Druids had many religious ceremonies, and some of them included human sacrifices. One writer described Stonehenge this way: "Though the day of the Druids is now long past and the cries of their victims no longer haunt the night, and the altar stone has ceased to drop blood, yet it is dangerous to go [to Stonehenge] when the sacrificial moon is full. For the Druids, by the blood they shed, their vile sacrifices and fellowship with the Devil, attracted forces of evil to the place . . . Shapeless invisible horrors haunt the vicinity and at certain times crave a resting place in a human body . . . ."

One of the important Druid ceremonies for their gods took place at the start of spring. Huge bonfires were lit. Then the Druids piled the bodies of animals and humans into a giant 50-foot high wicker dummy. *The dummy was then set on fire!*

Because the Druids held secret ceremonies, outsiders thought they had magical powers. Many legends have grown up about the Druids. One legend says that the stones of Stonehenge were really men who were transformed by the Druids.

There are a few hundred modern-day Druids in England and Wales, but modern Druids are not like the ancient Druids. They hold private meetings once a month to discuss religious subjects. Every Midsummer's Eve, busloads of Druids and carloads of tourists drive to Stonehenge for the Midsummer Druid Rites. The Druids dress up in white robes and walk among the giant stones, carrying incense, leaves, and baskets of bread. When the sun rises over the

Heel Stone, the ceremony and magic of the Midsummer's Eve is over.

Now that you have come full circle, you can make some guesses about Stonehenge. But with

Today many tourists attend the Druids' celebration.

the little evidence you have—some human ashes, crude tools, and the stones themselves—you still cannot know for sure what went on among the stones thousands of years ago. If the stones could speak, they would surely tell you some strange stories. Perhaps they might even tell you some of the secrets of our beginnings in the universe. With more scientific study, this just may happen. Anything is possible. For now, however, Stonehenge stands strong, silent, and mysterious on Salisbury Plain. Its secrets still lie buried in the stone giants that reach for the sky.